PIC ABC ISADORA
35251002113908
12y
Isadora, Rachel
City seen from A to Z

9 12
C   2

Discard

W9-ADQ-694

SOUTH MILWAUKEE PUBLIC LIBRARY
1907 TENTH AVENUE
SOUTH MILWAUKEE, WI 53172

Rachel Isadora
City Seen from A to Z

Greenwillow Books, New York

SOUTH MILWAUKEE PUBLIC LIBRARY
1907 TENTH AVENUE
SOUTH MILWAUKEE, WI 53172

Copyright © 1983 by Rachel Isadora
All rights reserved. No part of this book
may be reproduced or utilized in any form
or by any means, electronic or mechanical,
including photocopying, recording or by
any information storage and retrieval
system, without permission in writing
from the Publisher, Greenwillow Books,
a division of William Morrow & Company, Inc.,
105 Madison Avenue, New York, N.Y. 10016.
Printed in the United States of America
First Edition   10 9 8 7 6 5 4 3 2

Library of Congress Cataloging in Publication Data

Isadora, Rachel.
City seen from A to Z
Summary: Twenty-six black-and-white drawings
of scenes of city life suggest words beginning
with each letter of the alphabet.
[1. City and town life—Pictorial works.
2. Alphabet] I. Title.
PZ7.I763Ci 1983   [E]   82-11966
ISBN 0-688-01802-5
ISBN 0-688-01803-3 (lib. bdg.)

For James,
with more than love

Art

Beach ball

Car wash

Dolls

Entrance

Friends

Gallery

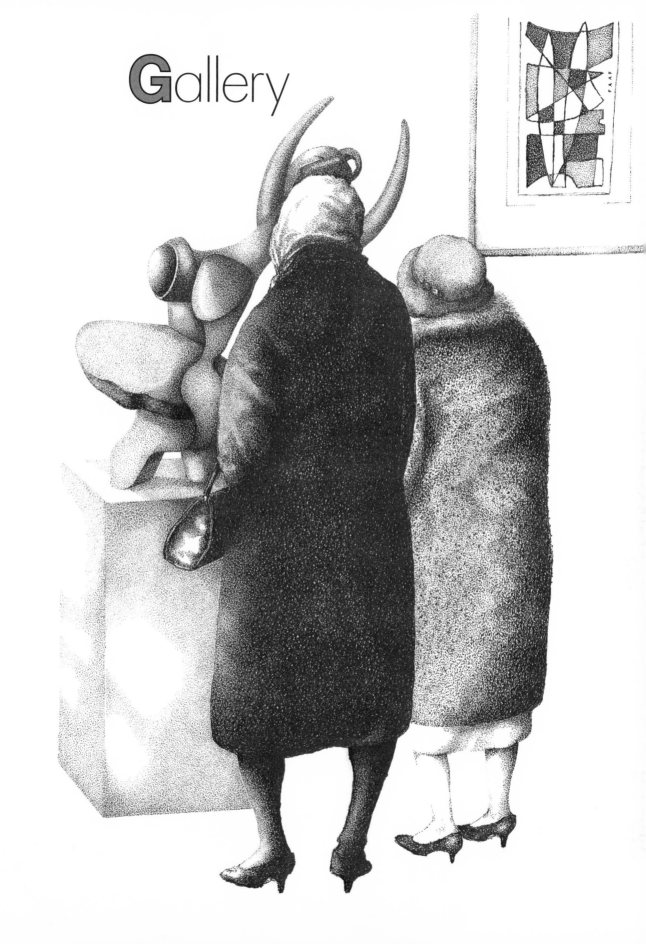

Hat

Ice cream

Jazz

Kitten

Lion

Music

Ocean

Pigeon

Quiet

Roller skates

Snowman

Tutu

Umbrella

Valentine

Window box

Xmas

Yoyo

Zoo

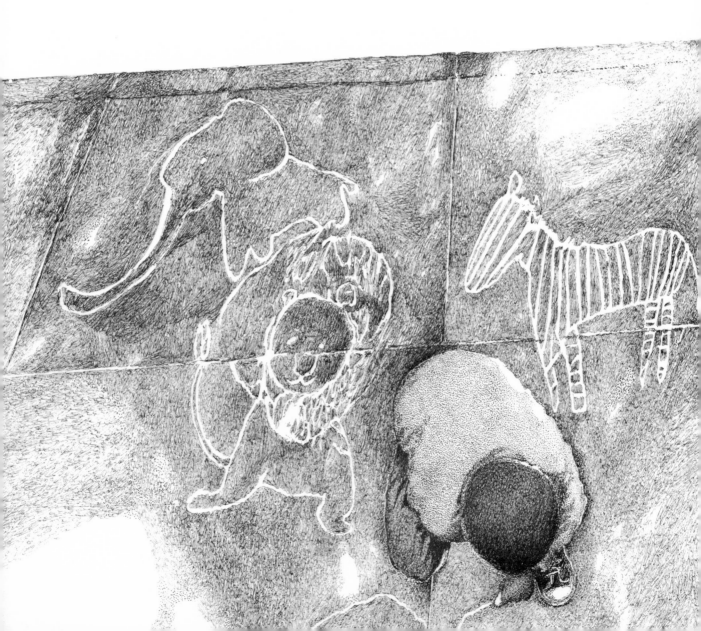